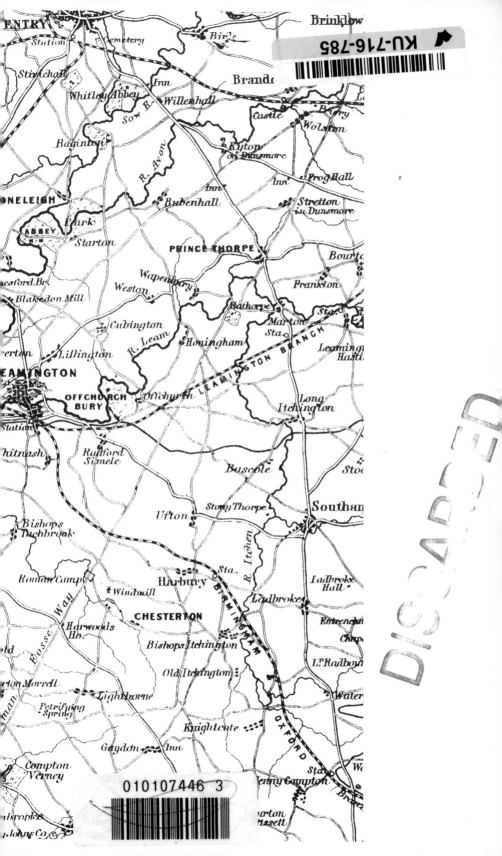

Bedford's Warwickshire 1987
has been published
in a Limited Edition
of which this is

Number 317

A list of original
subscribers is printed
at the back of
the book

Bedford's
WARWICKSHIRE

FRONT COVER: Warwick Castle from the River Avon.

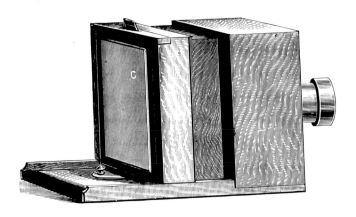

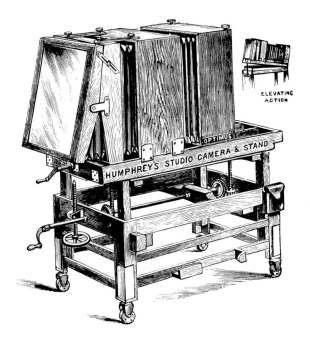

ELEVATING ACTION

Two cameras spanning the critical period of photographic development, from the 1850's 'box within a box', to the sophisticated studio apparatus of Queen Victoria's Jubilee year. Francis Bedford first published photographs in 1855 and served his final year on the Council of the Photographic Society in 1877.

Bedford's WARWICKSHIRE

A RECORD OF THE 1860s

BY

JOHN H. DREW MA FRSA

BARRACUDA BOOKS LIMITED
BUCKINGHAM, ENGLAND
MCMLXXXVII

PUBLISHED BY BARRACUDA BOOKS LIMITED
BUCKINGHAM, ENGLAND
AND PRINTED BY
LEICESTER PRINTERS LIMITED
LEICESTER, ENGLAND

BOUND BY
CAMELOT PRESS PLC
SOUTHAMPTON, ENGLAND

JACKET PRINTED BY
CHENEY & SONS LIMITED
BANBURY, OXON

LITHOGRAPHY BY
MRM GRAPHICS LIMITED
WINSLOW, ENGLAND

TYPESET BY
SWIFTPRINT
BUCKINGHAM, ENGLAND

© John H. Drew 1987

ISBN 0 86023 295 6

Contents

A NEW SERIES OF

STEREOSCOPIC AND ALBUM VIEWS,

ALSO

PANORAMIC AND CABINET PICTURES.

By FRANCIS BEDFORD,

PHOTOGRAPHER TO H.R.H. THE PRINCE OF WALES.

Illustrating the Scenery and Attractions of

LEAMINGTON,	KENILWORTH,
GUY'S CLIFF,	COVENTRY,
WARWICK,	STRATFORD-ON-AVON,
WARWICK CASTLE,	CHELTENHAM,
STONELEIGH,	TEWKESBURY,

PUBLISHED BY

CATHERALL AND PRICHARD, CHESTER.

Sold by GEORGE F. DEW,

At his PICTURE GALLERY, 32, BATH STREET, LEAMINGTON.

A catalogue of Francis Bedford's work, one of
two survivals. The overprint of his Chester
agent is on the cover.

Introduction

What was popularly know as leafy Warwickshire in the nineteenth century has developed into a thriving county of bustling towns, connected by heavily used roads which pass through a countryside of farms with close-clipped hedges. The early photographs in this book clearly reveal the transformation that has taken place.

Guy's Cliffe house (earlier spelt Cliff) is now a ruin, Kenilworth Castle is no longer a farmyard, the Earls have sold Warwick Castle and departed, while the mill beneath its walls no longer grinds corn. Charlecote House belongs to the National Trust, Stoneleigh Abbey has been put on the market (autumn 1986), Guy's Cliffe mill no longer grinds corn and several churches have disappeared from the Leamington Spa landscape. The Hathaways have left Shottery, and the cottage now belongs to the Shakespeare Birthplace Trust which also tends the Birthplace with great care.

Despite such a transformation, I doubt whether many of us would wish to exchange the benefits of today for the conditions of a century-and-a-quarter ago. The declining economic face of agriculture in the late nineteenth century, coupled with the social upheaval of two World Wars have ensured that those days have gone for ever. We are looking at a moment in time through the expert camera of Francis Bedford during his visits to Warwickshire, chiefly in the 1860s. His sales were aimed at a social class with some money and leisure and therefore the photographs reflect that requirement. However, it remains an invaluable historical document and a record of a now past style of living.

It was fascinating to find a number of photographs in which Bedford's son appeared in his low-crowned bowler. His wife also appears in a few. This was helpful in establishing the authenticity of some of the photographs.

Finally, I would like to thank Miss Pamela G. Roberts, Librarian, The Royal Photographic Society, for sparking off the idea for this book and for providing information; Mr D. V. E. Royall and Mr Roger Warren for reading the manuscript and Mr William Boswell for his professional services in copying originals; also Robin Bayliss for his excellent work in copying several Bedford photographs, and his jacket portrait. Thanks are also due to the Librarians at Kenilworth, Leamington Spa, Stratford-upon-Avon and Warwick for providing the facility for the limited edition of this book.

Kenilworth
1987

The Hunt Portrait of Shakespeare with frame
made from timber from the Birthplace. Now
discredited, it was discovered in 1860 by the
Town Clerk, William Oakes Hunt. Its
discovery a few years before the photograph
was taken would doubtless have influenced
Bedford. It is owned by the Shakespeare
Birthplace Trust. Bedford's picture comes
from his *Photographic Views of Warwickshire*.

Victorian County

There was a great resurgence of interest in Warwickshire during the first half of the nineteenth century, primarily through the attraction of Royal Leamington Spa as a leisure resort, the highly successful romance, *Kenilworth*, by Sir Walter Scott, and the Shakespeare revival which culminated in the purchase of the Birthplace for £3,000 after a public appeal in 1847. The congenial rural atmosphere of the county exercised a certain appeal, enhanced by the improved mode of travel following the coming of the railways in the 1840s.

Royal Leamington Spa, the then prime tourist centre, started as the small village of Leamington Priors, situated on the south side of the River Leam, with a population of 315 in 1801. By the time that Francis Bedford took his photographs it had increased to some 19,000 people and had assumed its present name. Speculators had begun to develop the south-sloping north side of the river, the river having been suitably widened to a respectable size through a series of weirs. Wide streets, with grandiose houses, hotels, attractive shops, subscription libraries and places of entertainment were quickly provided. Some prospered but a contemporary, Dr. A. B. Granville, noted in about 1840 that many quickly went out of business. In truth, the spa town only just made it, for fashion had by then decreed that Society should go to the seaside or abroad. The railway had helped sustain its popularity and Bedford, fortunately for us, took his camera to the town at that critical time. The affluent tourist either stayed at one of the wide range of hotels or rented accommodation, and usually hired a landau for excursions to such essential tourist spots as Kenilworth and Warwick Castles, Stoneleigh Abbey and Guy's Cliff and often combined several on the same day.

Stratford-upon-Avon had good hotels but little else to offer visitors once they had seen the Shakespeare properties. Its population did not increase with the dynamism of Royal Leamington Spa, despite an attempt to establish its own spa at Bishopton in 1840 and named 'the Victoria Spa', with the Queen's permission. There was not the investment in Stratford-upon-Avon. However, attempts were made to promote an attractive image long before the successful national appeal to purchase Shakespeare's Birthplace in Henley Street. The Shakespeare Club was founded at the Falcon Inn in 1824 and at a second attempt, in 1827, Stratford mounted a festival which attracted 40,000 people, clearly most of them being visitors. The Tercentenary of Shakespeare's birth in

1864 gave added impetus, though the small Shakespearean theatre which adjoined New Place garden was hardly a success during its lifetime. The legendary connection with Shakespeare stealing deer at nearby Charlecote was also an obvious attraction. However, modern research has cast serious doubts on this tale.

The Castles at Warwick and Kenilworth were further attractions, Warwick with its magnificent situation and because it was a home, and Kenilworth through Scott's novel. Indeed, no fewer than 20,000 visitors attended Mr Bunn's Revels of Kenilworth Castle on 13 and 14 August 1855 - he was lessee of the Theatre Royal Drury Lane and Covent Garden - most of them coming by way of the London and North Western Railway, which was 'materially fed by those of the Great Western Line'. The Stratford festival of 1827 and this Kenilworth example clearly show that people would travel, given a good enough reason, the first before the railway and the second afterwards. Stoneleigh Abbey had the added attraction of having been visited by Queen Victoria.

The socially conscious visitor was not interested in streets of old houses as we are today, but rather in the great houses and their families, castles and some lesser homes if they had substantial literary connections. One only has to look at the medieval city of Coventry, which was already being demolished, when such houses were thought to be unfit for habitation and new roads were driven through the ancient city, although, a few people did visit some of the more interesting industries. Miss Berry recorded in her diaries a visit to Mr Francis Littleton's horn comb factory at Kenilworth and thus provided a unique insight into that hand-crafted process.

Those who clamoured for mementoes of their visits looked to the photographers who supplied portraits and views. Many views were mundane, a few of a high standard. Francis Bedford's were of the latter, and he exploited the market by producing fine sets of photographs for the popular tourist sites. After all, the collecting instinct had a long tradition. The sepia albumen prints of the day were only 3″ x 3″ and the paper on which they were printed very flimsy. They were needle sharp but relied on available light for indoor views. Indeed, one photograph shows that a deep-carved plaque was carried outside for better lighting at Warwick Castle. Bedford placed characters in his views to improve the pictorial effect but the same people recur, particularly his son and occasionally his wife.

Some of the photographs had faded with the passage of time and therefore made reproduction of doubtful value, one being of the Kenilworth Buffet at Warwick Castle which had a splendid portrait of Queen Elizabeth above it.

Of the photographs reproduced here, the set of Guy's Cliff House is of the greatest historical value, for the house was deliberately gutted in the late 1940s. Similarly, the fine rooms of Warwick Castle were faithfully recorded well before the disastrous fire of 1871. Kenilworth Castle is shown as a working farm and Guy's Cliff Mill when it still ground corn. Fortunately Bedford also recorded some of the pleasant small villages, such as Ashow with its beautiful church overlooking the River Avon. We are privileged to have a glimpse at another world through the lens of Francis Bedford.

The First Photographers

For centuries artists had taken hours, sometimes years, to complete a painting of a landscape or a portrait of some long-suffering sitter, but photography quickly changed that situation. Painting did not die but rather took on a new lease of life. Like the first paintings, the early attempts at photography were crude. Improvements came swiftly.

Thomas Wedgwood, son of Josiah Wedgwood the celebrated potter, undertook a series of experiments, as did Sir Humphrey Davy, on the copying of images by the action of light on silver nitrate, and he published a report on his findings in 1802. However, the images were impermanent.

Nicephore Niepce, a French lithographer, was also conducting experiments and in 1826 produced the first image from a camera, though he had produced images since 1814. He later collaborated with Louis-Jacques Daguerre, a Frenchman, who announced his process in January 1839 and published it in September 1839, six years after Niepce's death, thus establishing one of the first popular forms of photography. The daguerreotype process necessitated the coating of a polished copper plate with silver oxide which, after being exposed in a camera, was developed in mercury vapour at 60°C (140°F) and then fixed to remove the unexposed silver oxide. The exposure took up to an hour, an arduous experience for those sitting for portraits. The cameras weighed up to 150lbs, and multiple copies were not possible since there were no negatives.

W. H. Fox Talbot (1800-1877) had taken his first photographs in 1834 and 1835 with a simple camera, which he had developed from the *camera obscura*, a device popular with artists, and which he had used for sketching during his tour abroad in 1833. Talbot was a man of many interests and seems to have been unaware of others working in competition. He was certainly disturbed to find that Daguerre had announced his findings first and so, with some urging, he published the results of his work in February 1839 following a lecture to the Royal Society a few days earlier. Talbot patented his calotype in 1841 and followed it with three further patents in later years. He was the inventor of the negative-positive process, which used paper coated with chloride and potassium bromide and became known as the calotype, later to be called the Talbotype. The print was obtained by passing the light of the sun through a paper negative on to sensitised paper. Positive prints could be taken in large quantities for the first time. Talbot had used writing paper for the early negatives and thus problems arose with the increasing opaqueness of the paper over a period of time. From 1848, glass took over from paper. There were complaints that Talbot's patents were hindering progress in the art, and so he relaxed them following court action. One cannot but wonder whether Frederick Scott Archer's work, announced a year earlier, could also have had a bearing on the decision. His process, known as the wet collodion process, used a mixture of pyroxylin (guncotton) and ether with the plate being exposed while still wet. Its great advantage was that exposure time was considerably shorter, and the photographer was able to travel provided he took his darkroom with him. Some leading photographers were known to use horse-drawn caravans.

Albumen paper, involving the white of eggs became popular, having been introduced by L. D. Blanquart-Evrard in May 1850. This was a slow and tedious way of producing prints, some reports mentioning only three a day from a negative.

By the late 1860s silver prints had fallen from popularity since they were prone to fade, and carbon took their place. Earlier that decade, stereoscopic views (first discussed by Charles Wheatstone in 1832 and perfected by Sir David Brewster in 1851) were available by several of the rival processes; hand-held cameras were introduced; the word *photography* had been coined years previously in 1839 by Sir John Herschel, who had also first used the word *snap-shot* in the 1860s. Herschel and others had for several years also been interested in the possibility of colour photography.

The wet-plate problem was not solved until 1871, when Dr Richard Leach Maddox introduced a gelatine emulsion. Within a decade George Eastman had introduced celluloid film.

Francis Bedford

Francis Bedford had witnessed these rapid developments and had a practical knowledge of the processes, which he used with the greatest skill and artistry. He was also well acquainted with his peers in the photographic world.

He was a quiet and retiring man, yet he enjoyed a distinguished career in photography and lithography during the Victorian years. His nature belied his intense activity and energy. Thus it is through his work that we begin to understand the man.

It has been established that Francis Bedford was descended from an old Cornish family whose records go back at least 500 years. The family name was Tubb and was centred in St Neot, Cornwall, though they seem to have left for London early in the seventeenth century. Bedford's grandfather, John Tubb, of Acton Green, Middlesex, arranged for the name to be changed to Bedford and it was promulgated in the *London Gazette* of May 1785 as granting a change of name 'in compliance with the request of his Uncle, the Rev Thomas Bedford of Letterkenny', Donegal, an Englishman, rector of Clonderaddock and a wealthy bachelor. Clearly he wished to perpetuate the family name and for his wealth to remain in the family.

Coming from such a family background, the immediate pressure to seek a living was not so urgent. Bedford's father, Francis Octavius Bedford, born in 1784, the year before the family change of name, married Sophia Curtis who bore him a family of five children, the two daughters of which died when quite young. Francis was the oldest of the three sons and was born in Southampton Row, Bloomsbury, London, in 1816. He became part of a large family of architects, solicitors, clergymen and several admirals.

Bedford married and lived for the remainder of his life at 326 Campden Road, north London, where the large garden permitted him ample space to erect his studios and processing rooms. His son, William, worked with his father and later took over the active running of the business. However, he died some sixteen months before his father after having contracted typhoid.

There remains some uncertainty about Bedford's early career, but it seems most probable that he joined the family architectural practice at an early age, for he is recorded as having exhibited nine architectural drawings between 1833 and 1849 at the Royal Academy, London (his father exhibited six between 1814 and 1832), the church at Turnstall was his first commission. His creative interest in lithography was already established by 1840, by when he was publishing work, initially on a small scale. Bedford gained large-scale commissions for several important books, the first large one being for *The Industrial Arts of the Nineteenth Century*, by Sir M. D. Wyatt in 1851, which included 160 of his lithographs of exhibits displayed at the Great Exhibition. However, Bedford had already become interested in photography.

In the 1840s photographic books on the new art began to appear which must have attracted his attention. Bedford's first recorded publication was for *The Photographic Album for the Year 1855*, which consisted of contributions from the members of the Photographic Club. Having a circulation of around 50 copies and with original photographs, the book was of limited circulation and therefore only publicised to members and not the general public, who were beginning to purchase photographs in increasing quantities.

Bedford received his first Royal commission from Queen Victoria in 1853 - to make a photographic panorama of Coburg which she wished to give to Prince Albert. The following year he received a further Royal commission, to photograph selected objects belonging to the Royal collection at Marlborough House. He photographed a further eleven items in 1855.

Stereoscopic pictures, mounted on card, were produced from c1860 and became popular. Bedford entered the market and produced several series including North and South Wales, Devon, Bristol, and Clifton, Kenilworth Castle, etc. Records show that he produced as many as 800 prints from a single negative, thus indicating the pressure of demand and the need for him to adapt his processes to meet large volume business. Doubtless he employed assistants at this stage.

The introduction of the collodion process had enabled Bedford to become more mobile: hence his stereoscopic views. He was not alone in making full use of the new mobility. Francis Frith went to Egypt and travelled 800 miles up the Nile between September 1856 and July 1857, taking huge negatives, some being 16 x 20 inches and others 8 x 10 inches, and he later paid a visit to Africa, Arabia and Palestine. Roger Fenton recorded the Crimean War under patronage of Queen Victoria. Magnificent records were taken of the building of *The Great Eastern* steam ship, of its designer on site, and of the building of the Crystal Palace. Bedford also made an extended foreign tour to the Middle East which set the seal on his career and his work.

The Royal Tour

Prince Albert, an ardent advocate of the arts and sciences, was no less keen on the education of his own children. Shortly before his early death in December 1861, he had planned a tour of the Middle East for the heir to the throne, the Prince of Wales (Edward VII), to complete the latter's formal education. The young Prince was to be accompanied by a small party of friends and officials which included his brother Prince Alfred, the Hon Robert Henry Meade, who was a highly experienced traveller and groom of the bed chamber to the Prince of Wales, General Robert Bruce as an old friend and confidant who was in charge of the party, Col Teesdale, Col Keppell, Dr Minter as physician and Dr Arthur Stanley, the scholar, who became Dean of Westminster in 1864. The death of Prince Albert did not delay the start of the tour and on the eve of departure the Queen, who was then at Osborne House, asked that Bedford should join the party as photographer.

They left in February 1862, staying in Germany and Austria *en route* to Venice where HMS *Osborne*, the Royal Yacht, awaited them. They arrived in Alexandria on 24 February for three weeks in Egypt, followed by the Holy Land, which they reached on 31 March. It was the first visit by an English prince since that of Edward 1. They later visited Syria, Constantinople, Rhodes and Athens. The party returned in mid-June with only one serious mishap. General Bruce contracted a serious illness in Jordan and died shortly after his return. The General had done much to make the tour a success and was successful in gaining permission for Bedford to photograph the Holy sites for the first time. Not only did Bedford have little time before leaving to collect the massive amount of equipment he needed, including chests of chemicals and glass plates, but he had a minimum of time to take and process negatives during the tour. The distances he covered were staggering considering that most leading photographers used a caravan as a portable darkroom.

Despite the pressures, which some critics had earlier said would be too much for Bedford's fastidious attention to detail, he positioned people and animals in his carefully composed pictures for the maximum photographic effect. This care gained the public's admiration on his return. In all, Bedford took 210 plates, of which 175 were subsequently published (48 of Egypt, 76 of the Holy Land and Syria and 48 of Constantinople, the Mediterranean and Athens). The Prince of Wales took a personal interest in Bedford's activities and welfare. At Hebron he asked Bedford to remain behind to take additional photographs and provided him with 50 soldiers to ensure his safety. Indeed, the only mishap of the tour occurred when an Arab porter accidentally smashed one of the huge plate cameras while carrying it up a rock. Prince Alfred, already an enthusiastic amateur, assisted Bedford in many ways, including cleaning the plates and focussing the negatives.

There was considerable interest in the methods used by Bedford during his tour in a warm climate. A contemporary report stated that he used Dr Hill Norris's plates which gave excellent results during the early part of the journey but noted that he encountered problems through the temperature changes and so subsequently confined himself to the wet process. For that he used Ponting's collodion and a stock of Tomas's bromo-iodized with pyrogallic acid development. He took fairly long exposures of 30 seconds despite the high intensity of the light, to enable him to bring out the black shadows. The development was stopped before the entire density of the sky was obtained. Bedford's negatives were taken on 12″ x 10″ plates using a single lens Ross and a Grubb. He had tested a Ross 8½″ x 6½″ orthographic lens at Ely Cathedral during the previous June. However, the intense heat presented a major problem since the plates were frequently partially dry before they could be developed but he overcame the problem by using a weak pyro developer. Bedford also experienced considerable problems with the plagues of small flies adhering to the plates and buzzing around the interior of the camera. Sand was simply ignored. It is astonishing that he achieved such fine results after having experienced so many problems. On his return to London, Bedford was able to take greater care in the preparation of the prints, yet only four weeks after his return, in July 1862, he mounted a major exhibition of the tour at the German Gallery, Bond Street.

The Prince of Wales and the touring party immediately paid a visit. Contemporary reports laid lavish praise on the exhibition, one stating that it was 'unquestionably the finest series of Eastern photographs', and noted 'a marvellous stereoscopic effect in the architectural views', the perfection of the half-tones and that there were 'no hard skylines so noticeable [as] in [other people's] Oriental photographs'. The catalogue had an introduction by M. W. Thompson in which he described the overpowering effect of the photographs as vast and grand. The ensuing publications were by no means cheap. It was said, during the exhibition, that the photographs would be published in 21 parts, each containing 8 or more illustrations. The bound copies of three volumes sold for 43 guineas. A cheap edition followed in 1867, with only 48 photographs. Francis Bedford was immediately recognised as the undoubted leader in his field. He was not only a fine photographer, but also an innovator and inventor.

A Professional Touch

Bedford was a member of The Photographic Society virtually from its inception, joining in 1857. He was quickly nominated to its Council, at the meeting held on 21 December 1857, and remained on the Council until 1887. He was elected a Vice-President at the Annual General Meeting held in 1878, at the meeting at which the death of W. H. Fox Talbot was also announced. Although only three of his articles were published in the *Transactions*, they revealed aspects of his inventiveness, such as his proposal for an instantaneous shutter and for suitable glass for darkroom windows. He also tested new equipment and sometimes travelled some distance to do so, as when testing a Ross 8½″ x 6½″ orthographic lens at Ely Cathedral. Bedford was also the first person to make good use of electric light in his printing (1861). Recognition came from overseas such as the silver medal at the 1867 Paris Universal Exposition.

In 1878 Bedford seconded a motion, at his Vice-Presidency meeting, which sought to further the progress of photography, by offering prizes to 'successful competitors in an examination in technical photography' which was run conjointly with the (Royal) Society of Arts.

Francis Bedford's business grew to a size which was beyond his own capabilities so he appointed Catherall and Pritchard, Eastgate Row, Chester as his main agents. Their catalogues of his photographs were published and distributed throughout the country, often with the name of local sellers overprinted on the covers. It appears that other local publishers also used his negatives. For example, the name of H. T. Cooke & Son, of Warwick, publishers of local guide books etc, appears in the margins of some of Bedford's Warwickshire prints.

Francis Bedford died at 1.45pm on Tuesday 15 May 1894 at the age of 78, 'A veteran photographer; full of years and full of honours' and was buried in Highgate Cemetery the following Saturday.

The Photographic Journal, 26 May 1894 also paid its tribute, stating that 'His work, which is too well known to need more than a passing allusion, was frequently to be seen in the Society's Exhibitions, where it, on more than one occasion, secured an award. Landscape photography, and more particularly landscape photography of that kind which may be described as typically English, was the direction in which his work lay, and it was without doubt the marked ability he exhibited in this direction, that led to his selection to accompany HRH The Prince of Wales during his tour in Palestine and the Levant in 1862.' And so the quiet and retiring master photographer passed into history leaving the valuable legacy of his achievement.

Francis Bedford began his career in the family architectural practice, then used his creative talents to turn to lithography with immediate success, and finally to follow what was then a natural progression into the new and exciting world of photography. In each aspect of his career he applied himself at a high professional level of competence that quickly attracted recognition. His managerial skills must have been of an equally high standard. The peak was reached in the recognition of his work in landscape photography, where his meticulous attention to detail in the composition of his pictures and in the processing of the negatives and prints earned him universal praise. He attracted international honours which extended beyond those of his rivals, and he remained the professional photographer after those rivals retired. While others had also been invited to photograph treasures belonging to the Royal Family, it was he who was selected to accompany the Prince of Wales on his educational tour abroad and thereby secured his pre-eminence.

There was nothing to detract from his achievement. Even today, we are grateful to him for recording so much of the Victorian age for us to enjoy. His photographs often tell so much more of that age than can be recorded in words.

The *raison d'être* for this book is to bring together almost all of his known Warwickshire work from the fragile faded sepia original prints for a renewed appreciation of his achievement.

19

How It Was Done

H. Baden Pritchard gave a unique insight into the processing used by the various leading photographers in 1883. He was impressed by the great pains that Francis Bedford took in preparing his prints. He visited the studio and noted the process used, recording that after toning and fixing, the prints were individually agitated by hand to free them from the hyposulphite and were then passed through a series of troughs each with water flowing from the previous trough. The prints were then left in a large washing trough for 18 hours, resting on a lattice work under which, in winter, was a serpentine tube through which passed hot water to enable the washing to be held at a tepid temperature. A little water wheel, which revolved once a minute, filled little buckets and caused a crank to turn and a 'flapper' to agitate the water and the prints. There was also a long arm in the water to control its level and to check the water wheel.

Bedford was prudent in his business and careful not to waste expensive materials resulting in not less than 75% of the silver expended in the printing being recovered. From the hyposulphite solutions Bedford reckoned that he recovered half as much of the silver as from the first washing waters. The first three wash waters were supposed to contain all the silver salt that was worth collecting and so the silver was recovered by pouring them down a sink in a corner of the room. That was connected by a rubber tube to three large earthenware pans, each holding 60 gallons and embedded in sawdust for protection against frost and accidental breakage. Each pan was filled in turn, and, when the first was filled, hydrochloric acid was added and then left to stand. By the time the other two were filled the chloride of silver in the first had precipitated. It was then drawn off and filtered through flannel and sent to the refiners who, as manufacturing chemists, converted it into nitrate.

The sensitizing room was equipped with facilities for 'exciting' and drying 120 sheets of paper at a time. Four huge baths of nitrate of silver were arranged in a row on a low dresser after which the paper was put over a drying rod. A long wheeled trough was placed underneath the wet sheets to receive the falling liquid. Printing was mostly done under glass. A linen screen was pulled across the windows when the sun shone as Bedford had found that the sashes left their shadows on the pictures.

Every negative was edged in black paint so as to present a white margin and also to reduce his costs. Bedford said that the deep black edges in an ordinary print used as much gold as the picture itself. Finally, the negative number was written on the margin.

The skies were improved in the negatives and the horizon softened. Detail was sometimes also added to the foreground. Earlier he had covered parts of the negative with tracing paper and worked with pencil or brush on it. He observed that tracing paper became yellow with time and also opaque, which then revealed its outline. To overcome the problem he ground the reverse side of the glass negative by means of a glass muller (stone) and emery powder, which secured a good surface upon which he could work. He made free strokes with a brush dipped in Indian ink or with a pencil. The grinding of the glass behind the horizon line, sea or hills, tended to soften the plate considerably.

Such was the attention to detail paid by Francis Bedford to score over his rivals and receive the critics' compliments. His studio was in reality an early example of the modern production line. The record of his methods also reveals the enormous demand for photographs.

Bedford's Books

A wide variety of sources have been searched for the work of Francis Bedford, including the British Museum and Victoria and Albert Museum Catalogues. *The Incunabula of British Photographic Literature,* Helmut Gernsheim (Scholar Press, 1984) was a particularly useful source of information, and the reader is referred to that book for more detailed information of several items mentioned. For some unknown reason the number of photographs included in several of the publications varied. For example, the late Warwickshire album of photographs varied between 15 and 18 sepia prints in a luxurious publication where the photographs were mounted on heavy card, the endpapers were of an expensive paper and the thick covers of green cloth were heavily embossed with the gold lettering of the title and ornamental surround. Francis Bedford's publications were by no means cheap tourist books.

Some publications were undated and the author has accordingly given an approximate date. Helmut Gernsheim has acribed 1865-1875 for the albums at the end of the list, but from the Warwickshire prints in particular there is an indication that they were taken within the earlier part of this ascribed period.

Of additional importance is the collection at the Birmingham Public Libraries which purchased the Francis Bedford Collection in 1985. It comprised some 3,000 glass negatives and prints together with the Frith Collection of some 310,000 negatives. The Library also holds the manuscript catalogue of his negatives.

Society of Dilettanti: Ionian Antiquities III, Sir W. Gell, J. P. Gandy, F.Bedford, 1840 lithog.

A Chart Illustrating the Architecture of Westminster Abbey, c1840 4to./folding plate

Sketches in York, nd, probably c1840. 14 lithog.

The Churches of York, 1843, W. Monkhouse and F. Bedford with historical &c notes by the Rev J. Fawcett. Plates with letterpress.

A Chart of Anglican Architecture: arranged chronologically with examples of the different styles, 1843, publ. York

A Chart Illustrating the Architecture of Westminster Abbey, 1846, 1 tinted lithog., folding 4to.

The Industrial Arts of the Nineteenth Century, Sir M. D. Wyatt, 1851. 160 lithog. by Francis Bedford. A series of illustrations of specimens from many countries which were exhibited at The Great Exhibition

The Photographic Album for the Year 1855, being contributions from the members of the Photographic Club, 1855. 44 albumen prints with text including Francis Bedford and Roger Fenton.

A Chart of Anglican Church Ornament,wherein are figured the saints of the English Kalendar with their appropriate emblems, the different styles of stained glass, and various sacred symbols and ornaments used in churches. Collected from ancient examples, 1856. 1 lithog., folding, partly coloured 8vo.

The Grammar of Ornament ... one hundred ... plates, drawn on stone by Francis Bedford, 1856. Renaissance and Italian periods.

Examples of Ancient Doorways and Windows, arranged to illustrate the different styles of Church Architecture from the Conquest to the Reformation, from existing examples, 1856. 1 lithog. folding 8vo.

The Photographic Album for the Year 1857, being contributions from the members of the Photographic Club, 1857. 39 albumen prints with contributions by Francis Bedford, Roger Fenton and others. Both the 1855 and 1857 albums were limited to c 50 copies.

The Sunbeam, a Photographic Magazine, 1857. Issued in 5 parts from January 1857 with 4 albumen prints in each issue. Francis Bedford contributed.

Treasures of the United Kingdom from the Art Treasures Exhibition, Manchester, 1858. Edited by J. B. Waring. Chromo-lithographed by Francis Bedford.

The Sunbeam, a Book of Photographs from Nature, 1859. The 1857 edition republished complete. With contribution by Francis Bedford.

The Photographic Art-Annual 1859. Originally issued in parts, 18 albumen prints in each, including contribution by Francis Bedford.

Gems of Photographic Art. Photo-pictures, selected from the Universal Series by Francis Frith, c1862. Includes 6 albumen prints by Francis Bedford.

Ruined Abbeys & Castles of Great Britain, Wm and Mary Howitt, 1862. 27 plates including some by Francis Bedford and Roger Fenton.

Photographic Pictures made by Mr Francis Bedford during the Tour in the East, in which, by command, he accompanied HRH The Prince of Wales. 1863. 4 vol.

Photographic Pictures made by Mr Francis Bedford during the Tour in the East in which, by command, he accompanied HRH The Prince of Wales, 1863, 3 vols. of 172 albumen prints.

The Wye: Its Ruined Abbeys & Castles, Wm & Mary Howitt, 1863. With 6 photographs, 4 being by Francis Bedford (republished from Ruined Abbeys & Castles of Great Britain)

Photographic Pictures of Egypt, the Holy Land & Syria, Constantinople, the Mediterranean, Athens, etc., 1863. 4pp

Ruined Abbeys & Castles of Great Britain, Wm & Mary Howitt, 1864. Volume 2 of the book first published in c1862. 26 plates

Frith's Photo-Pictures, 1864. First issued to subscribers at 15 photographs a year and over 4 years.

History of the recent Discoveries at Cyrene, made during an Expedition to the Cyrenaica in 1860-61 under the Auspices of Her Majesty's Government by Capt R. Murdoch Smith and Commander E. A. Porcher, c1864. 16 photographs and lithographs by Francis Bedford.

The Ruined Castles of North Wales, Wm & Mary Howitt, c1864. Some photographs by Francis Bedford. Republished from *Ruined Abbeys & Castles of Great Britain*.

Our Inheritance in the Great Pyramid, Charles Smyth, c1864. 5th edition 1890. Frontispiece of Great Pyramid by Francis Bedford.

The Grammar of Ornament, 1865. A folio of 112 plates drawn on stone by Francis Bedford of the Renaissance and Italian periods. (See first edition of 1856)

Examples of Ornamental Art in Glass and Enamel, ed. J. B. Waring, c1866 with 18 chromo-lithographs by Francis Bedford.

*Photographic Pictures made by Mr Francis Bedford during the Tour in the East ...*1867. 48 photographs of smaller size in a popular edition.

The Stones of Palestine. Notes of a ramble through the Holy Land, Mrs M. Nott, c1867. 12 albumen prints by Francis Bedford.

The Holy Land, Egypt, Constantinople, Athens ...tour in the East, c1867. Popular edition of the earlier expensive work of 1863.

A Poor Man's Photography at the Great Pyramid in the Year 1865, Charles Smyth, c1870

The following undated books consist of photographs and brief captions which probably dated post 1865:

Photographic Views of Bristol & Clifton, u/d, various edns, with up to 16 prints;*Photographic Views of Beddgelert*, u/d, 10 prints; *Photographic Views of Chester*, u/d, 10 prints; *Photographic Views of Devonshire*, u/d, 20 prints; *Photographic Views of North Devonshire*, u/d, 17 prints; *Photographic Views of South Devonshire*, u/d, 15 prints; *Photographic Views of Exeter*, u/d, 15 prints; *Photographic Views of Stratford-upon-Avon & its Neighbourhood*, u/d, 10 prints; *Photographic Views of Tenby & its Neighbourhood*, u/d, 16 prints; *Photographic Views of Torquay & its Neighbourhood*, u/d, (Helmut Gernsheim records two issues, one of 30 prints and one marked 'No 2' of 10 albumen prints); *Photographic Views of Warwickshire*, u/d, 15/18 prints;

Bedford's Warwickshire

LEAMINGTON SPA
Bath Street looking north. Waterloo House
(Nos 12 to 14) on left, which Edward Stone &
Co opened in 1850 as linen drapers and silk
mercers. Victoria Terrace in the distance.

ABOVE: Bath Street. The Post Office with six-columned portico opened in 1846. The shop, left, proclaims on its facade 'The only manufactory for the genuine Leamington salts'. OPPOSITE ABOVE: Victoria Terrace. On the corner one of the popular bazaars, booksellers and museums. Rows of small photographs and large prints are displayed and children's hoops hang in the adjoining doorway. LEFT: The Old Well, now destroyed. The first stone building was built over the earliest spring in 1803 and replaced ten years later by a more substantial building which was altered to form the one shown. To the left, L. Rochat's Warehouse (No 47), est 1850. RIGHT: Lower Parade at the corner of Dormer Place.

ABOVE: Euston Place looking north. The garden of
Denby Villa beyond, later to become the site for the
Town Hall. BELOW: Euston Place from across the
Parade.

ABOVE: The Parade. The Regent Hotel (left) whose foundation stone was laid on Saturday 18 July 1818, was completed a year later at a cost of £25,000. The porticoed entrance was added in 1849, the original being on the south face. BELOW: All Saints Parish Church from the Jephson Gardens, which replaced the ancient church enlarged several times. The nave was completed in 1844, the chancel in 1845, the north transept and clocktower in 1849 and the south transept in 1869, after the vicar, Rev John Craig, had initiated the scheme.

ABOVE: The Parish Church from the Mill Walk. LEFT: The Jephson Gardens from Victoria Terrace, taken over on 12 May 1846 as a memorial to Dr Jephson. RIGHT: Dr Jephson monument, Jephson Gardens. Dr Henry Jephson (1798-1878) was a remarkably successful doctor whose popularity contributed to the prosperity of the spa.

ABOVE: Victoria Bridge, built 1840 to replace an earlier, narrower one. The north end of Victoria Terrace beyond, built 1836-38. BELOW: Holly Walk and Brandon Parade, a continuation of Regent Grove.

29

ABOVE: The College (later Leamington College for Boys), formed 1845 for 'providing for sons of the nobility, gentry, and clergy, a sound classical and mathematical education, in accordance with the principles of the Established Church'. It was erected in 1847 at a cost of £6,000, the foundation stone laid by Dr Jephson. BELOW: The College - a portion of the principal front which is 155 feet long and forms the south wall of the hall.

Milverton Chapel and Church Hill, known as the
Pepper Box Chapel from the ornamental tower on its
roof. It opened on 5 August 1836 to accommodate 800.
The altar ceiling was groined and ornamented with
pilasters, between which were inscribed the Lord's
Prayer, Ten Commandments and Apostles' Creed. It
was demolished in 1883.

ABOVE: St Mary's Church, Radford Road, built on land given by Edward Willes before houses were constructed in its vicinity. It thus acquired the name of St Mary's in the Fields for half-a-century. Few attended the foundation stone laying ceremony on 5 October 1838, in protest at its siting. It was built remarkably quickly, being consecrated on 27 July 1839. BELOW: Lillington Church, dedicated to St Mary Magdalen, once belonged to the monks at Kenilworth. It was extensively restored in 1847, and enlarged in 1858 and 1868.

ABOVE: Ashow Church, from the village, dedicated to the Assumption of Our Lady. This delightful church stands on the bank of the River Avon, beyond the long, winding village street. Church Cottage (right). LEFT: Ashow Church. RIGHT: Emscote Church, All Saints, designed by James Murray and built 1854-56. Considerable additional work included the tower and spire, consecrated in 1872, indicating a later date for this photograph.

GUY'S CLIFFE

OPPOSITE ABOVE: The Avenue from the road. Guy's Cliffe, the place of legend, where Guy of Warwick retired and lived a hermit's life of prayer and devotion. His disguise was so successful that even his own wife did not recognise him and he only revealed himself to her at the point of death. Richard de Beauchamp, Earl of Warwick, built a chapel, dedicated to St Mary Magdalen, inside which is a huge stone statue of Guy, carved from the natural rock. The house is in ruins; the fine church still stands, although it has undergone restoration both inside and out. The main part of the house was built about 1751.BELOW: The house from the Mill Meadow. The River Avon flows beneath the wall. Older people recalled otters there. ABOVE: Avenue front, from the Garden.

ABOVE: West front, from the Avenue. The north and west sides were considerably altered by Percy Greatheed in the early 19th century. OPPOSITE ABOVE: The house from the Well Meadow. BELOW: View from the Garden Seat.

LEFT: The White Gateway. RIGHT: Courtyard, with the Great Cedar. The chapel is at the far end. BELOW: South front from the courtyard. The lancet windows (right) belonged to the kitchen built by Bertie Greatheed, which filled the space between house and chapel.

LEFT: The Chapel, originally of about 1422 but altered in the late 18th century. The tower dates from the mid-15th century. RIGHT: Guy's Statue, standing against the chapel wall, is over eight feet high. Traces of paintwork remain. An early directory states that it is 'in the attitude of drawing his sword; the right arm is wanting, and the left bears a shield, the hand of which had also gone'. A female sculptor replaced one of the missing legs in the early 19th century. BELOW: Rock stable and arches in the courtyard. The rooms are cut from the natural rock. Those shown here face the chapel. There are more rooms, off right. By the river is Guy's cave and nearby an enormous church-like cave with aisles.

Guy's well.

The Mill, Guy's Cliffe. There has been a mill on the site since at least the 12th century. Samuel Greatheed of Guy's Cliffe acquired it around 1780 when it was rebuilt. The wooden balcony was added in 1821.

OPPOSITE ABOVE: The bridge and fall, from the mill. The fall was lowered some years ago to help reduce flooding when the River Avon was in spate. BELOW: Gaveston's Monument. Piers Gaveston, the unpopular favourite of Edward II, was tried at Warwick Castle and executed on Blacklow Hill, near Guy's Cliffe, in 1312. The monument was erected in 1821, and bears the inscription 'In the hollow of this rock was beheaded, on the first day of July, 1312, by the barons as lawless as himself, Piers Gaveston, Earl of Cornwall, the minion of a hateful king, in life and death a memorable instance of misrule.' (The date should read 27 June). He was buried in the church at King's Langley in 1315 by order of the king. Dugdale recalled that a cross called Gaveston's Cross had stood near the top of the hill and that '1311, P. Gaveston Earl of Cornwall beheaded here' was cut into the rock. ABOVE: The Mill from the bridge.

WARWICK

St Mary's Church and Church Street. The nave, aisles and tower of the earlier church were destroyed in the fire of Warwick (5 September 1694). Much of the town centre was burnt down, and inhabitants were allowed to take salvaged furniture into the church. Unfortunately, some was smouldering, thus igniting it. The Beauchamp Chapel escaped with little damage. Rebuilding took place from 1698 to 1704 to designs by Sir William Wilson of Sutton Coldfield, although Sir Christopher Wren made some preliminary drawings. The tower is 174 feet high to the tops of the pinnacles. They were rebuilt in 1885. (Wren purchased nearby Wroxall Abbey in 1713).

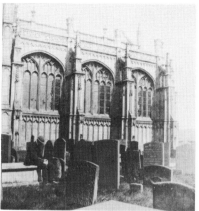

LEFT: The East Gate from Jury Street. It was already in existence by the late 14th century. The present chapel replaced an earlier one in 1788 and is dedicated to St Peter. RIGHT: Exterior of the Beauchamp Chapel, known also as the Chapel of Our Lady, completed in 1463 after 21 years. It was not consecrated until 1475. BELOW: Beauchamp Chapel, interior looking east. Almost in the centre is the magnificent tomb of its founder, Richard Beauchamp, Earl of Warwick, who died in 1439. The recumbent statue of latten rests on a base of Purbeck marble although it is not a likeness. To the right is the tomb of Ambrose Dudley, Earl of Warwick, died 1590, dressed in armour and wearing a coronet.

OPPOSITE ABOVE: The West Gate and Leicester's Hospital. The gate dates back to at least the 12th century, its tunnel being partly carved out of the living rock. The chapel was restored in 1863-5 by Sir Gilbert Scott at about the time of this photograph, before the east end was altered and the flying buttresses added to the south side. BELOW: Leicester's Hospital and Master's House. ABOVE: Leicester's Hospital, Porch and Gateway. The hospital was founded by Robert Dudley, Earl of Leicester, in 1571, for twelve poor men and the master. It had previously been the hall of the amalgamated guilds of St George and of the Holy Trinity and Blessed Virgin Mary, dating back to the reign of Henry VI.

47

OPPOSITE ABOVE: Leicester's Hospital, Entrance Gateway, from Quadrangle. The Burghers' Hall was at the top of the stairs (left). BELOW: The Old Ruined Bridge, from beneath the Castle wall, dated from the 14th century and was the earlier entrance to the walled town from the south. ABOVE: The Bridge, built 1789-93, to replace the ancient one, has a graceful arch of 105 feet span. BELOW: The Grist Mill and Castle. Rebuilt 1867-8 and destroyed by fire in 1880.

ABOVE: From the Bridge. One of the great views of England, looking down the River Avon to the imposing south front of the Castle. The mill stands beneath the wall (centre) together with the remains of the ancient bridge. BELOW: Entrance Gateway, from the outer court, dates from the 14th century, and Guy's Tower with the barbican projecting in front. OPPOSITE ABOVE: Gateway and Caesar's Tower, from the outer court. BELOW: Clock Tower from the inner court.

50

ABOVE: Guy's Tower (from the inner court) is 128 feet high and was completed in 1394. Its walls are ten feet thick. OPPOSITE ABOVE: Entrance Porch and Dining Room. The Great Dining Room was built by Francis, Earl of Warwick, about 1770. BELOW: The Mount and Keep Tower, partly hidden by trees. The motte is surmounted by two turrets. The tradition that Alfred the Great's daughter, Ethelfleda, erected the mound in 915 has been discounted.

OPPOSITE ABOVE: Exterior of Armoury, etc at the north-facing, west end of the residential part of the Castle. To the extreme left is part of the chapel, while partly hidden (centre) is a large tower containing a spiral staircase. BELOW: Caesar's Tower, and portion of the principal front; the east end of the residential part; the library to the right. Caesar's Tower was built between 1350 and 1370 by the first Thomas de Beauchamp. Seated on natural rock, it is four storeys and 147 feet high. Both Caesar's and Guy's Towers are machicolated. ABOVE: Principal front, from the Mount.

55

OPPOSITE ABOVE: Bear Tower, shown here, together with Clarence Tower to its west, were a part of Richard III's plan to build a massive tower (1483-5) some 80 by 65 feet in plan. It was the first residential guest tower in the County. BELOW: South Tower, from the Park, now called Watergate or Hill Tower. LEFT: The Warwick Vase, found on the bed of Lake Pantanelle at Hadrian's Villa, near Tivoli, Italy, in 1770, and purchased by George, second Earl of Warwick from his uncle, Sir William Hamilton. It is of white marble, standing 5′ 6″ high and 5′ 8″ in diameter. The pedestal is modern. The vase is said to have been considerably restored. It is now in Glasgow.

RIGHT: Cedars, from the Park. BELOW: View from the Castle balcony.

ABOVE: The Mill and Caesar's Tower.
OPPOSITE ABOVE: The rustic bridge in
the Park. BELOW: The old cedar tree.

OPPOSITE ABOVE: The Great Hall. Its ancient roof was replaced in 1830 with one in the Gothic Style (here), which was destroyed in the fire of 1871. The Hall measures 62' x 40' x 35' high. The present roof is considerably higher, thus revealing the clerestory windows once more. BELOW: Armour and cabinets in the Great Hall. ABOVE: The Dining Room, dating from the 18th century.

ABOVE: Chimney piece in the dining room. BELOW: The Kenilworth Buffet, in the dining room, was carved from the ancient oak from the Park and exhibited at the 1851 Great Exhibition. It is decorated with scenes from Sir Walter Scott's romance, *Kenilworth*. The buffet was purchased for £1,200 and presented to the Earl of Warwick, on his marriage, by the County. A portrait of Queen Elizabeth is above it.

The Red Drawing Room.

ABOVE: The Cedar Drawing Room. LEFT:
Passage to the armoury. RIGHT: The
armoury.

ABOVE: Bay window in the armoury.
BELOW: Wood carving, Battle of the
Amazons.

STONELEIGH ABBEY

ABOVE: The principal front, built 1714-26 by Francis Smith of Warwick, who also designed the Pump Rooms at Leamington Spa. Queen Victoria and Prince Albert visited the Abbey in 1858, shortly before this picture was taken. The Italian Garden was laid out by Chandos Leigh after 1839, when he acquired the title and estate as a gift from the Crown. OPPOSITE ABOVE: The north front. BELOW: The house, from the north-east.

OPPOSITE ABOVE: The old Gatehouse, 14th century. To the right the hospice where guests were received and entertained. BELOW: Entrance Gateway to the quadrangle. ABOVE: The garden.

The old oak in the Park. Possibly the enormous pollard oak of 33' girth which was near the Abbey. There was an unlikely tradition that William Shakespeare wrote one of his plays beneath it.

KENILWORTH

The following group is unique in that it shows the Castle before the debris from its destruction during the Civil War was removed. They also reveal the ruins before rebuilding and restoration post-1870. For example, we see the east wall of the Banqueting Hall before it was partly rebuilt and the buttresses built; the area between Gaunt's kitchens and the Keep, Lunn's Tower, etc before building work took place. Similarly, Leicester's Buildings where it was recorded that the north-west corner was temporarily 'shored up to resist the pressure of the ruinous, western face', the buttress walls to the west and north having been removed at various times, and 'the ill-built corner, being honey-combed with joistholes and fireplaces, cannot sustain the weight'. There were other works too, not least the removal of the farmyard. This record shows the scene as Sir Walter Scott saw it when writing *Kenilworth* (1821) and Charles Dickens in the summer of 1838, when he found it such a splendid 'summer resort'.

70

St Nicholas Parish Church, from the north-east, mainly 14th century but considerably altered. Its spire was rebuilt after being struck by lightning twice in one night in 1858.

LEFT: Norman doorway to the Parish Church. Pevsner wrote that it is 'the most sumptuous Norman doorway in Warwickshire'. RIGHT: The Abbey of St Mary, the Gateway, late 14th century. Founded as an Augustinian Priory by Geoffrey de Clinton, Chamberlain and Treasurer to Henry I, about 1122. Raised to Abbey status in mid-15th century. BELOW: The Castle Grove skirts the west side of the Brays.

The Castle from the brook, looking across the
ford, in those days part of the Welsh Road, an
old drovers' road.

ABOVE: View from near the Castle Inn (now Queen and Castle). Leicester's Gatehouse, later transformed into a home by Colonel Hawkesworth during the Civil War. The east wing was added in 1650. BELOW: The Gatehouse, north side. The route through the building was blocked by Tudor windows taken from Leicester's Buildings and the inside walls lined with Irish oak panelling.

Porch to Gatehouse.

OPPOSITE ABOVE: Alabaster chimney piece in Gatehouse, ground floor. Traces of the blue and gilt decoration survive. It was removed from the Castle, together with the unmatched overmantel. BELOW: Caesar's Tower from the wall. South view, Leicester's Buildings (left), with the two faces of the south-east corner, showing holes left by the great clock faces. Leicester, as part of his modernisation of the Castle, removed all but one of the small Norman windows and replaced them with huge, light-admitting windows. ABOVE: Leicester's Buildings, east front, built for the celebrated visit of Queen Elizabeth I in 1575.

OPPOSITE ABOVE: Caesar's Tower, south side. BELOW: Leicester's Buildings, from Caesar's Tower. ABOVE: Banqueting Hall, from Leicester's Buildings. Built by John of Gaunt, it occupies the west side of the inner court. Its upper floor was the hall, the lower the cellar, 90 x 45 feet. It was the first of its type with a hammer beam roof, and said to be the finest in the country. BELOW: Banqueting Hall, from Caesar's Tower, before the rebuilding of the east wall and addition of buttresses.

OPPOSITE ABOVE: Caesar's Tower, from
Banqueting Hall. BELOW: Entrance to
Banqueting Hall, upper level. ABOVE:
Mervyn's Bower.

Upper end of Banqueting Hall.

Interior of Banqueting Hall.

ABOVE: Fireplace in Banqueting Hall.
LEFT: Windows in east wall of Banqueting
Hall. RIGHT: Oriel Window, Banqueting
Hall, facing inner court.

LEFT: Banqueting Hall, from north-east.
The magnificent carved stone arch (left),
through which Leicester led Queen
Elizabeth to dine in 1575. RIGHT: Ruined
lobby and staircase. BELOW: Part of the
White Hall, late 14th century.

85

ABOVE: Leicester's Buildings from the moat. OPPOSITE ABOVE: Lunn's Tower, late 13th century. BELOW: The Gatehouse, from the farmyard.

ABOVE: Farm buildings: Leicester's Barn
(left) and Water Tower (right).   BELOW:
General view from the bridge.

88

STRATFORD-UPON-AVON

Holy Trinity Church from the lock gates on the River Avon. It was the first English river to be adapted for navigational purposes, and could take boats some 35 feet in length with pivoted masts to enable them to pass under the low bridges. The work was undertaken from 1636, taking three or four years to complete. Trade revived in the early 19th century through the corn-mills, near the church, but navigation was abandoned in 1875 by the Great Western Railway, who had earlier purchased the rights.

ABOVE: Holy Trinity from the River Avon, dates from the 13th century. The south aisle, about 1332, by John de Stratford. The chancel was rebuilt in the late 15th century, and the decayed wooden spire was replaced by the present one in 1764. BELOW: Clopton Bridge, built by Sir Hugh Clopton, late 15th century. He was Lord Mayor of London.

ABOVE: Anne Hathaway's Cottage, Shottery, dates back to at least the 15th century. During the 18th century it was divided into two and later into three dwellings. Further alterations were carried out in 1697. It was purchased for £345 from William Taylor, a descendant of the Hathaways, in 1838 by Thomas Barnes who bequeathed it to William Thompson. He sold it to the Trustees and Guardians of Shakespeare's Birthplace in Henley Street for £3,000 on 19 May 1892. BELOW: Charlecote, the principal front. Built of brick with some stonework, the house was begun in 1558 by Sir Thomas Lucy. Considerable work was carried out in the first half of the 19th century, including the building of the library and dining room in 1833. The estate belonged to the family for over 700 years, but passed to the National Trust in 1946. The fine herd of deer still roam the park, but the tradition that William Shakespeare was brought before Sir Thomas Lucy for poaching deer has been disproved. The garden, seen here, has since been replaced by a lawn. Dugdale showed it as a large ornamental pool.

ABOVE: The porch, part of the 1558 structure. The remodelled hall can be
seen (right). BELOW: North Wing and terrace gates. The gates were made
by Nicholas Parris of Warwick in 1772 and match a second pair adjoining the
south wing. Access to the River Avon, which runs in front of the west face of
the house, is gained by the footpath (right).

The following group of photographs were
published later than the preceding ones in
Photographic Views of Warwickshire. It was a
luxury volume with the photographs
mounted on thick card.

ABOVE: Leamington Spa, The Parade and
Regent Hotel. BELOW: Warwick Castle, the
inner court from the Mount.

ABOVE: Warwick Castle, the Cedar
Drawing-room, looking east. BELOW:
Guy's Cliffe from the Mill.

ABOVE: Stoneleigh Abbey from the river
bank. BELOW: Kenilworth Castle from the
bridge.

ABOVE: Kenilworth Castle, Leicester's Buildings and Caesar's Tower. BELOW: Kenilworth Castle, the Banqueting Hall.

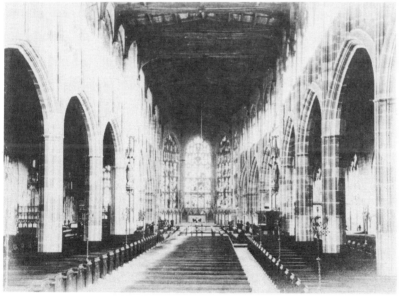

ABOVE: Coventry, from Greyfriars' Green.
BELOW: Coventry, St Michael's Church
(later Cathedral), interior looking east.

97

ABOVE: Stratford-upon-Avon. Holy
Trinity Church from the north-east.
BELOW: Stratford-upon-Avon. Holy
Trinity Church, the Chancel.

98

ABOVE: Stratford-upon-Avon. William Shakespeare's
Birthplace, from the east. BELOW: Stratford-upon-
Avon. Shakespeare's Birthplace, the room in which the
poet was born.

99

ABOVE: Anne Hathaway's Cottage, Shottery. BELOW AND OPPOSITE: Three views by Bedford, all early, but those of the Kenilworth Castle Gatehouse and Abbey Gatehouse bear the imprint of H. T. Cooke & Son, Warwick: Banqueting Hall, Kenilworth Castle; Gatehouse, Kenilworth Castle; Abbey Gateway, Kenilworth.

ABOVE: A stereoscopic view by Bedford, c1860. Kenilworth Castle from the south. BELOW: Guy's Cliffe House, Avenue front, which is probably not by Bedford but complements his views of the house. As an architectural record it contrasts sharply. OPPOSITE: Facsimile pages from Francis Bedford's Catalogue, one of two surviving examples.

103

Unmounted.	C. D. V.	Slides.	No.		Unmounted.	C. D. V.	Slides.	No.

C. D. V.
Slides.

Unmounted.

C. D. V.
Slides.

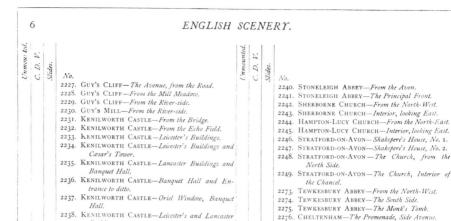

Unmounted.	C. D. V.	Slides.	No.		Unmounted.	C. D. V.	Slides.	No.
			2227. GUY'S CLIFF—*The Avenue, from the Road.*					2240. STONELEIGH ABBEY—*From the Avon.*
			2228. GUY'S CLIFF—*From the Mill Meadow.*					2241. STONELEIGH ABBEY—*The Principal Front.*
			2229. GUY'S CLIFF—*From the River-side.*					2242. SHERBORNE CHURCH—*From the North-West.*
			2230. GUY'S MILL—*From the River-side.*					2243. SHERBORNE CHURCH—*Interior, looking East.*
			2231. KENILWORTH CASTLE—*From the Bridge.*					2244. HAMPTON-LUCY CHURCH—*From the North-East.*
			2232. KENILWORTH CASTLE—*From the Echo Field.*					2245. HAMPTON-LUCY CHURCH—*Interior, looking East.*
			2233. KENILWORTH CASTLE—*Leicester's Buildings.*					2246. STRATFORD-ON-AVON—*Shakspere's House, No. 1.*
			2234. KENILWORTH CASTLE—*Leicester's Buildings and Cæsar's Tower.*					2247. STRATFORD-ON-AVON—*Shakspere's House, No. 2.*
			2235. KENILWORTH CASTLE—*Lancaster Buildings and Banquet Hall.*					2248. STRATFORD-ON-AVON—*The Church, from the North Side.*
			2236. KENILWORTH CASTLE—*Banquet Hall and Entrance to ditto.*					2249. STRATFORD-ON-AVON—*The Church, Interior of the Chancel.*
			2237. KENILWORTH CASTLE—*Oriel Window, Banquet Hall.*					2273. TEWKESBURY ABBEY—*From the North-West.*
			2238. KENILWORTH CASTLE—*Leicester's and Lancaster Buildings.*					2274. TEWKESBURY ABBEY—*The South Side.*
			2239. KENILWORTH CASTLE—*Interior of Banquet Hall.*					2275. TEWKESBURY ABBEY—*The Monk's Tomb.*
								2276. CHELTENHAM—*The Promenade, Side Avenue.*
								2277. CHELTENHAM—*The Proprietary College.*
								2278. CHELTENHAM—*The College Gymnasium.*

THE ALBUM CABINET PICTURES.

A NEW SERIES *of* PHOTOGRAPHIC VIEWS *by* F. BEDFORD. PRICE ONE SHILLING EACH.

Average Size, 5¾ by 4. On Mounts, 10 by 7¼.

Unmounted.	Mounted.	No.		Unmounted.	Mounted.	No.
		265. In the Castle Grove, Kenilworth.				594. Leamington, View in the Jephson Gardens.
		266. Entrance to the Glen, Kenilworth.				595. Tachbrook Church, near Leamington.
		267. Flemish Wood Carving at Warwick Castle.				596. Whitnash Church, Interior of Chancel.
		268. Mill on the Avon, at Stratford.				597. Warwick and St. Mary's Church.
		269. Room in which Shakspeare was born.				598. Warwick, St. Mary's Church and Church Street.
		270. Charlcote.				599. Warwick, West Gate and Leicester's Hospital.
		271. Tewkesbury Abbey, looking East.				600. Warwick, Leicester's Hospital, Principal Front.
		272. Tewkesbury Abbey, looking West.				601. Warwick, Leicester's Hospital, the Master's House.
		528. Kenilworth, from the Brook.				602. Warwick, Leicester's Hospital, Interior of the Chapel.
		529. Kenilworth Castle, from the Meadow.				603. Warwick, Beauchamp Chapel, Interior, looking East.
		530. Kenilworth Castle, General View from the Bridge.				604. Warwick, Beauchamp Chapel, Interior, looking West.
		531. View at Kenilworth.				605. Warwick, Beauchamp Chapel, Leicester's Monument.
		532. Warwick Castle, from the Bridge.				606. Warwick, the Castle Mill on the Avon.
		533. Warwick Castle, General View.				607. Warwick Castle, General View.
		534. The Warwick Vase.				608. Warwick Castle, from the Bridge.
		535. The Avenue, Guy's Cliff.				609. Warwick Castle, from the Avon.
		536. Guy's Cliff, from the Mill Meadow.				610. Warwick Castle, from the Park.
		537. Southam, near Cheltenham.				611. Warwick Castle, the South Front.
		538. Seven Springs, near Cheltenham.				612. Warwick Castle, Cæsar's Tower and Mill.
		591. Leamington, Lower Parade and Regent Hotel.				613. Warwick Castle, Gatehouse and Cæsar's Tower, from the Outer Court.
		592. Leamington, the Parish Church, from Bath Street.				614. Warwick Castle, General View, from the Outer Court.
		593. Leamington, the Parish Church, from the Jephson Gardens.				615. Warwick Castle, the Inner Court, from the Mount.
		593*. Leamington, the Parish Church, from the Jephson Gardens. Near View.				616. Warwick Castle, Gatehouse and Cæsar's Tower, Inner Court.

Unmounted. *Mounted.*

No.

617. Warwick Castle, Guy's Tower and Gatehouse, Inner Court.
618. Warwick Castle, Principal Front and Cæsar's Tower.
619. Warwick Castle, the Principal Front, from the Mount.
620. Warwick Castle, Guy's Tower and Walls.
621. Warwick Castle, the Cedars of Lebanon.
622. Warwick Castle, the Great Hall, No. 1.
623. Warwick Castle, the Great Hall, No. 2.
624. Warwick Castle, Armour in the Great Hall.
625. Warwick Castle, the State Dining Room.
626. Warwick Castle, the Red Drawing Room.
627. Warwick Castle, the Cedar Drawing Room, No. 1.
628. Warwick Castle, the Cedar Drawing Room, No. 2.
629. Warwick Castle, the Gilt Drawing Room.
630. Warwick Castle, the Queen's Toilet in State Bedroom.
631. Warwick Castle, the Boudoir.
632. Guy's Cliff, the Avenue, from the Road.
633. Guy's Cliff, from the River-side.
634. Guy's Cliff, from the Mill.
635. Guy's Cliff, Guy's Well.
636. Guy's Cliff, Guy's Cave.
637. Guy's Mill, from the Road.
638. Guy's Mill, from the River Bank.
639. Kenilworth Castle, from the Bridge.
640. Kenilworth Castle, from the Echo Field.
641. Kenilworth Castle, from the South-East.
642. Kenilworth Castle, from the Village.
643. Kenilworth Castle, from the Road.
644. Kenilworth Castle, from the Inner Court.
645. Kenilworth Castle, Leicester's Buildings and Cæsar's Tower.
646. Kenilworth Castle, Front of the Banquet Hall.
647. Kenilworth Castle, Leicester's and Lancaster Buildings.
648. Kenilworth Castle, Lancaster Buildings and Banquet Hall, No. 1.
649. Kenilworth Castle, Lancaster Buildings and Banquet Hall, No. 2.
650. Kenilworth Castle, Entrance to Banquet Hall.
651. Kenilworth Castle, Interior of Banquet Hall.
652. Kenilworth Castle, Cæsar's Tower, from Banquet Hall.

Unmounted. *Mounted.*

No.

653. Stoneleigh Abbey, from the River-side.
654. Stoneleigh Abbey, the Principal Front.
655. Coventry, the Three Spires, from the Green.
656. Coventry, Tower and Spire of St. Michael's.
657. Coventry, Interior of St. Michael's, looking East.
658. Coventry, Interior of St. Michael's, looking West.
659. Coventry, Interior of St. Michael's, from the Aisle.
660. Coventry, the Sculptured Reredos, St. Michael's.
661. Coventry, Holy Trinity Church, from the South-east.
662. Coventry, Holy Trinity Church, Interior, looking East.
663. Coventry, the Gray Friars Hospital.
664. Sherborne Church, from the North-West.
665. Sherborne Church, Interior, looking East.
666. Hampton-Lucy Church, from the North-East.
667. Hampton-Lucy Church, Interior, looking East.
668. Stratford-on-Avon, Shakspere's House, No. 1.
669. Stratford-on-Avon, Shakspere's House, No. 2.
670. Stratford-on-Avon, Ann Hathaway's Cottage, Shottery.
671. Stratford-on-Avon Church, from the North-East.
672. Stratford-on-Avon Church, Interior of the Chancel.
673. Stratford-on-Avon Church, Shakspere's Monument.
674. Stratford-on-Avon Church, Clopton Chantry & Chancel.
743. Tewkesbury, High Street and Old Houses.
744. Tewkesbury Abbey, from the West.
745. Tewkesbury Abbey, the South Side.
746. Tewkesbury Abbey, Interior of the Choir, looking West.
747. Cheltenham, the Promenade Drive, looking up.
748. Cheltenham, the Promenade Drive, looking down.
749. Cheltenham, the Promenade Drive, the Central Avenue.
750. Cheltenham, the Promenade Drive, the Side Avenue.
751. Cheltenham, the Queen's Hotel.
752. Cheltenham, Royal Wells Walk and Spa.
753. Cheltenham, St. Mary's (the Parish) Church.
754. Cheltenham, Proprietary College, Principal Front.
755. Cheltenham, Proprietary College, the Chapel.
756. Cheltenham, Proprietary College, Interior of the Chapel.
757. Cheltenham, Proprietary College, the Gymnasium.
758. Cheltenham, the High Street.
759. Cheltenham, Pittville Spa and Lake.
760. Cheltenham, Pittville Spa, the Pump Room.
761. Cheltenham, the Devil's Chimney, Leckhampton.

MINIATURE VIEWS. (TWELVE ON A CARD.)

PRICE SIXPENCE, AND ONE SHILLING EACH.

1s. *6d.* *No.*

62. Coventry.
63. Stratford-on-Avon.
65. Leamington, Guy's Cliff and Stoneleigh.
66. Warwick and Warwick Castle.

1s. *6d.* *No.*

67. Kenilworth.
68. Cheltenham and Tewkesbury.
69. Worcester.

CABINET PICTURES.

A Series of PHOTOGRAPHIC VIEWS *by* F. BEDFORD.   PRICE TWO SHILLINGS AND SIXPENCE EACH.

Average Size, 8¼ by 6¼. On Mounts, 14¼ by 10¼.

No.
9. Warwick Castle, from the Avon, No. 1.
12. Beauchamp Chapel, Interior, looking East.
13. Tombs in Beauchamp Chapel.
14. Monument to the Earl of Leicester, Beauchamp Chapel.
17. Stratford-on-Avon Church, Interior of Chancel, No. 1.
285. Guy's Cliff, the Avenue, from the Road.
286. Guy's Cliff, the House, from the Avon.
287. Guy's Cliff, the House, from the Mill Meadow.
288. Guy's Mill, from the Avon.

No.
289. Warwick Castle, from the Bridge.
290. Warwick Castle, the River Front, from the Park.
291. Warwick Castle, from the Avon, No. 2.
292. Beauchamp Chapel, Interior, looking East.
293. Kenilworth Castle, from the Bridge.
294. Kenilworth Castle, from the Echo Field.
295. Stratford-on-Avon, Shakspere's House.
296. Stratford-on-Avon, the Church.
297. Stratford-on-Avon Church, Interior of Chancel, No. 2.

CARD SIZE PICTURES. (SIXPENCE EACH.)

(Continued from Catalogue Part 2, Page 2.)

No.
79. LEAMINGTON—*Lower Parade and Regent Hotel.*
80. WARWICK—*Leicester's Hospital, Interior of the Chapel.*
81. PEEPING TOM AT COVENTRY.
104. TEWKESBURY—*High Street and Old Houses.*
105. TEWKESBURY ABBEY—*From the West.*
106. TEWKESBURY ABBEY—*The South Side.*
107. TEWKESBURY ABBEY—*Interior of the Choir, looking West.*
108. CHELTENHAM—*Promenade Drive, looking up.*

No.
109. CHELTENHAM—*Promenade Drive, looking down.*
110. CHELTENHAM—*Promenade Drive, the Central Avenue.*
111. CHELTENHAM—*Promenade Drive, the Side Avenue.*
112. CHELTENHAM—*The Parish Church.*
113. CHELTENHAM — *Proprietary College, Interior of the Chapel.*
114. CHELTENHAM—*The High Street.*
115. CHELTENHAM—*Pitville Spa and Lake.*

CHESTER, HEREFORD, WELLS, EXETER, LICHFIELD, GLOUCESTER, ELY, PETERBOROUGH, LINCOLN, ST. DAVID'S, &c. ILLUSTRATED,

In a Series of PHOTOGRAPHIC VIEWS *by* F. BEDFORD.

PRICE FIVE SHILLINGS EACH.

Average Size, 11 by 9 inches. On thick Mounts, 20¼ by 14¼.

No.
81. Beauchamp Chapel, Warwick, Earl of Leicester's Monument.

No.
82. The Cedars in Warwick Park, No. 1.
83. The Cedars in Warwick Park, No. 2.

Sources

Francis Bedford

The British Journal of Photography
Journal of the Photographic Society
The Photographic Journal
The Photographic News
The Times
The Photographic Studios of Europe, Piper & Carter, 2nd edn, 1883
The Bulletin of the University of New Mexico, No 7, 1973
Masters of Victorian Photography, John Hannavy, 1976
Photography: the first 80 years, exhibition catalogue, London, 1976
The Photograph Collector's Guide, Lee D. Witkin & Barbara, London, 1979
Creative Camera, No 186, December 1979
Incunabula of British Photographic Literature, Helmut Gernsheim, 1984
The Golden Age of Photography 1839-1900, edit. M. Haworth-Booth, V & A
   Catalogue, 1984

The photographs

Antiquities of Warwickshire, Sir William Dugdale, 2nd edn., 1780
The Victoria County History of the County of Warwick
Transactions of the Birmingham Archaeological Society
A New and Complete History of the County of Warwickshire, William Smith,
   1829
Spas of England, A. B. Granville, Vol 2, 1841
The Journals and Correspondence of Miss Berry, 1865
The Castle of Kenilworth, Rev E. H. Knowles, 1872
Black's Guide to Warwickshire, 1866
Shakespeare's Land, C. J. Ribton-Turner, 1893
Ward Lock & Co's Leamington, Warwick, Kenilworth, etc, 1907
Warwickshire, Nikolaus Pevsner & Alexandra Wedgood, 1966
Shakespeare's Lives, S. Schoenbaum, 1970
A Manor of the King, John H. Drew, 1971
The Book of Royal Leamington Spa, John H. Drew, 1978
The Archaeological Journal, Vol 142 for 1985, 1986

Figures in *italics* refer to illustrations.

Index

Subscribers

Presentation Copies

1 Warwickshire County Council
2 Kenilworth Library
3 Warwick Library
4 Leamington Spa Library
5 Stratford-upon-Avon Library
6 Royal Photographic Society

7 John H. Drew MA FRSA
8 Clive & Carolyn Birch
9 Mrs Jennie Drew
10 Mrs J. M. Bostock
11 Mrs S. R. Jones
12 Miss B. V. Mash
13 Brian & Dorothy Daly
14 D. H. Boyce
15 Mr & Mrs F. E. Gould
16 Miss Amy Jayne Hornblow
17 Mr & Mrs T. G. Hornblow
18 Mr & Mrs P. S. Puddifoot
19 Mrs J. M. Grant
20 G. R. Key
21 C. G. & V. N. Raine
22 Cyril Hobbins
23 Margaret Hughes
24 Miss J. Gardner
25 Michael Thomas Bowles
26 Mrs Rosemary Elliott
27 Andrew Hall
28 J. S. S. Sterry
29 J. Lancaster
30 D. A. White
31 W. F. P. Merriman
32 T. R. Fancott
33 Mrs E. Brown
34 Winifred Minns
35 James L. Perkins
36 Peggy & Arthur Wakefield
37 Mrs P. Hornby
38 Mrs S. Robinson
39 Victoria & Albert Museum
40 London Guildhall Library
41 Miss J. M. Perkins
42 Mrs B. F. Rolf
43 Celia Rickers
44 Irene & Peter Thomas
45 David Dalton
46 Joan & Herbert Heydon
47 Mrs Irene Stearn
48 Philip J. Holloway
49 Mr & Mrs R. D. Gardner
50 Mrs M. E. Everitt
51 Mrs D. J. Sheepy

52 Mr & Mrs R. A. Hosking
53 Betty & Stanley Barratt
54 Mrs D. R. Forsyth
55 G. Watkins
56 Mrs Norma Claymore
57 I. D. Stant
58 R. L. Miller-Mead
59 R. M. B. Kenyon
60 P. G. Hardisty
61 Derek Nash
62 Mrs I. Edmunds
63 Paul & Carole Kelly
64 Miss D. L. Shaw
65 D. G. Hollings
66 M. Edmond
67 Mrs P. D. Harris
68 Barry Shiers
69 Janet Shiers
70 Deena Blundell
71 Barbara & Clive Underhill
72 Mr & Mrs J. D. Sanders
73 Mrs M. B. Hurst
74 J. A. Lord
75 R. A. Cheeseman
76 Mrs H. G. Manning
77 C. M. Foster
78 Warwickshire County
   Record Office
79 Mrs M. Woolley
80 Leslie James
81 A. Cork
82 Mrs Kathleen Hurst
83 M. George
84 Mr & Mrs D. F. Field
85 D. E. Smith
86 Mrs H. Prowting
87 M. Lloyd-Smith
88
   Leslie James
89
90 Mr & Mrs J. Marr
91 R. W. Palmer
92
   John H. Drew MA FRSA
93
94 Alfred Ernest Wright
95 Mary & Derek Dwyer

96 Margaret & Roy Bedford
97 Michael Lancaster
98 Robert C. Parnell
99 Barry Job
100 Chris Corby
101 Alison Sharp
102 Derek Eccles
103 T. W. Slater
104 Mr & Mrs J. P. Ash
105 The Trinity School,
106   Leamington Spa
107 St Paul's CE School,
      Leamington Spa
108 Dr G. E. Grice
109 Simon C. E. W. Hryhoruk
110
    T. Field
111
112 Christine Morris
113 Mrs K. B. Oakley
114
    Roy Wilkinson
115
116 T. J. J. Capnerhurst
117 John M. Labrum
118 G. G. Blunt
119 Mrs E. M. Eades
120 I. P. Cousins
121 D. B. Lockhart
122 P. J. Coulls
123 Robin Groves
124 John R. Fortnum
125 Shirley Strachan
126 Simon Jonathan Bennett
127 Mark James Bennett
128 Mrs J. D. M. Sheepy
129 J. E. Leonard
130 Lady Hamilton
131 Ann Donnelly
132 J. McKenzie
133 Mark Graham
134 G. P. Lovelock
135 L. S. Thompson
136 V. M. Griffin
137 T. & J. A. Palmer
138 R. J. Chamberlaine-Brothers
139 Major Eric Davies
    FRIBA MRTPI

111

140	B. G. Norman	199	Mrs D. A. Robotham	263	Mrs Celia Cox
141	Paul Briggs	200	R. R. Key	264	C. W. Mee
142	Paul Morgan	201	A. Newton	265	Roy Bourne
143	Alan W. Field	202	R. I. Wall	266	Warwick Castle Ltd
144	Philip Banham	203	T. G. Gardner	267	P. N. Meggitt
145	Anthony Charles Talliss	204	Mrs B. White	268	Harold Alan Carr
146	Mrs M. Smith	205		269	Doris Butcher
147	Mrs J. E. Crutchfield	214	Solihull Public Libraries	270	Terence G. Gardner
148	Robin A. Richmond	215	Mrs I. N. Harvey	271	E. E. Bissell
149	Ena Bradley	216	Mrs Flora Wood	272	Warwickshire Museum
150	Hilary David	217	Amy B. MacDonald	273	Jane R. Fellows
151	Mrs G. M. Reynolds	218	C. S. Hudson	274	June Colston
152	Beryl Blount	219	G. W. Harris	275	Meryl Nunn
153	Peter Milne	220	Keith John Kerton	276	P. D. Davies
154	Trevor Jones	221	Peter K Morrell	277	Grahem E. Cooper
155	Tony & Rosemary Watts	222	Ken & Yvonne Lines	278	Mrs Kathleen M. Dealtry
156	Mrs Barbara Miles	223	Vivian A. M. Hoffman	279	J. H. Baldwin
157	T. B. Freeman	224	Adrian Macdonald	280	Mark & Diana Barnard
158	Margaret Hughes	225	David William Grindrod	281	Philip M. Day
159	Emily Wills	226	Mr R. & Mrs J. E. Bayliss	282	C. H. Adams
160	Mrs I. V. Clegg	227	Mrs Susan Legge	283	Mrs J. M. Duffy
161	P. & J. Capper	228	Joan Bolton	284	Peter & Jane Deverill
162	Gordon Greenley	229	E. M. Hemming	285	Mrs P. Tarver & Family
163	A. G. Ballinger	230	Mr & Mrs J. R. Pickstock	286	Judith Coote
164	Miss Sheila M. Fitzgerald	231	Alan Robinson	287	Guy R. Atkin
165	John Richard Scurrell	232	Mr & Mrs Lionel Hunt	288	Jenni Fuller
166	K. G. Teague	233	Mrs A. Jarolim		
167		234	Mr & Mrs David Rodgers	289	L. F. Ekins
168	Anne Burgess	235	Miss Eileen A. Rodgers	290	P. Faulks
169	John Hadley	236	Mr & Mrs A. J. W. Pearson-	291	W. C. Bishop
170	David W. Cooper		Smith	292	P. S. London
171		237	Mrs Yvonne Kennedy	293	John & Carol Hubbard
172	W. Woodcock	238	Robert & Dawn Pearce	294	C. H. Bryant
173	Betty Gibson	239	Dr John W. Busby	295	J. D. Kaye
174	Mrs Judith Coltman	240	Coventry City Library	296	Mrs E. Higgins
175	Margaret Rushton	241		297	R. A. Key
176	Lynn Godfrey	242	Dorothy Stuart-Heatherley	298	B. S. Knight
177	Oliver Furley	243	M. J. O'Callaghan	299	Robert Hawthorne
178	James D. McPhillips	244	David D. Clarke	300	Val Tole
179	R. A. Norton	245	Miss N. M. Lucas	301	Albert J. Thomas
180	H. R. Moses	246	Conrad Davis	302	Westwood Library,
181	Alan G. Griffin	247	Roger Warren		University of Warwick
182	D. W. Burge	248	Paul Morgan	303	John Ivens
183	J. Gabryliszyn	249	Roger Smith	304	Mrs W. F. Harvey-Madeley
184	Mark Bunford	250	Jasmine Edlin	305	B. R. E. Cox
185	M. A. F. Small	251	Coventry Lanchester	306	Monica J. Stow
186	D. G. Poulton		Polytechnic	307	Mrs V. M. Brown
187	Mrs D. L. Butcher	252	W. H. Adams	308	Warwickshire County
188	B. S. Knight	253	Colin Parker	362	Library
189	G. Warwick	254	Maud Elizabeth Cox	363	The Librarian, Southam
190	Marilyn M. Lowe	255	Campion School,		School, Leamington Spa
191	R. A. Richmond		Leamington Spa	364	A. A. Hunter
192	Mr & Mrs H. T. Collett	256	A. Hewins	365	John H. Drew MA FRSA
193	Mr & Mrs M. A. Todd	257	Eric W. Norman	366	De Montfort Hotel
194	Mr & Mrs G. Collett	258	David Nason		
195	N. Collett	259	Andrew C. McWilliam		
196	J. Paveley	260	Mrs Joyce Callender		
197	Mrs M. G. Bagley	261	Miss Maisie Harris		
198	K. Twissel	262	Lillian Margaret Harris		*Remaining names unlisted.*

ENDPAPERS: Section of a map of Warwickshire taken from *Black's Guide to Warwickshire*, 1866.